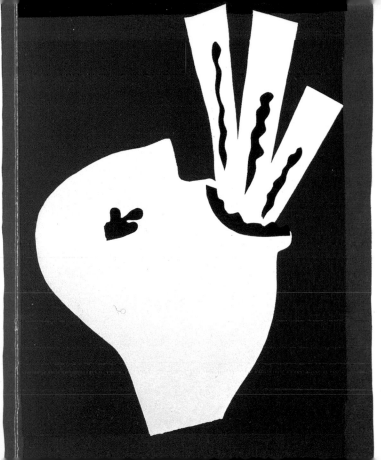

W9-BZP-947

# MATISSE
## *A POSTCARD BOOK*™

*Running Press*
*Philadelphia, Pennsylvania*

*Postcard Book* is a trademark of Running Press Book Publishers.

Canadian representatives: General Publishing Co., Ltd., 30 Lesmill Road, Don Mills, Ontario M3B 2T6. International representatives: Worldwide Media Services, Inc., 115 East Twenty-third Street, New York, New York 10010.

9  8  7  6  5  4  3  2  1
The digit on the right indicates the number of this printing.

ISBN 0-89471-711-1
Cover design by Toby Schmidt.
Interior design by Robert Perry.
Cover illustration: *Blue Nude III,* 1952, by Henri Matisse. Private collection (Giraudon/Art Resource, New York).
Back cover illustration (detail): *Icarus,* from *Jazz,* 1943, by Henri Matisse. The Estate of Matisse (Art Resource, New York).
Title page illustration: *The Clown,* from *Jazz,* 1938, by Henri Matisse. School of Fine Arts, Paris (Giraudon/Art Resource, New York).

Typography by Commcor Communications Corporation, Philadelphia, Pennsylvania.
Printed and bound in the United States of America by Innovation Printing, Philadelphia, Pennsylvania.
This book may be ordered by mail from the publisher. Please add $2.50 for postage and handling for each copy. *But try your bookstore first!* Running Press Book Publishers, 125 South Twenty-second Street, Philadelphia, Pennsylvania 19103

***W***hen Henri Matisse wrote in 1908 that he strove for "an art of balance, of purity and serenity. . .something like a good armchair in which to rest," his words seemed a bit odd: just three years earlier the French art world had begun to call Matisse and several of his contemporaries Fauves, or "wild beasts," because of their unconventional use of color.

The inconsistency between Matisse's mild words and the critics' scornful epithet revealed the tension between the artist's innovation and his audience's expectations. Matisse had abandoned a law career in 1891 to become a serious student of the master painters. When he began to lean toward neo-impressionism and the work of Cézanne, the critics were shocked.

Fauvism represented an advance on impressionism. Abandoning conventional color theory, Matisse chose colors to convey a sensation, a feeling of "the moment." The viewer could have the pleasure of "a good armchair" and, at the same time, a truer representation of reality than meticulous detail alone could convey.

The prestigious exhibition where the Fauves made their debut, the 1905 Paris Salon d'Automne, marked the beginning of Matisse's relationship with an influential group of patrons led by Gertrude Stein and her family. At the Steins' Paris home, Matisse met an international group of collectors who were much more receptive to his works than were their French counterparts.

Matisse was now able to support his growing family as he continued to define his art. While other Fauves began to explore cubism, Matisse chose an independent path. During the next five decades he shifted between realism and abstraction, Fauvism and classicism. The decorative detail of Islamic art and the spare technique of Japanese drawing, the brilliant Mediterranean light of Nice and the exotic costumes of Morocco all found their way into Matisse's interiors, still lifes, and portraits.

By mid-century Henri Matisse was considered, with Picasso, one of the two great artists of the age; but perhaps more satisfying to the artist, his work began to be acclaimed in his native France. More than forty years after his controversial Fauvist debut, Matisse was named Commander of the Legion of Honor. The wild beast had finally tamed his greatest critics.

*STILL LIFE WITH APPLES*
1897, by Henri Matisse (French, 1869–1954). Oil on canvas.
Private collection. (Art Resource, New York)

*A GLIMPSE OF NOTRE DAME*
*IN THE LATE AFTERNOON*
1902, by Henri Matisse (French, 1869–1954). Oil on paper
mounted on canvas, 72.5 × 54.5 cm. Albright-Knox Art
Gallery, Buffalo, New York: Gift of Seymour H. Knox, 1927.

## NUDE IN THE STUDIO

1904, attributed to Henri Matisse (French, 1869–1954).
National Museum of Modern Art, Paris. (Giraudon/Art
Resource, New York)

MATISSE  A Postcard Book™
© 1989 by Running Press Book Publishers

## VIEW OF COLLIOURE

1905, by Henri Matisse (French, 1869–1954). Oil on canvas.
Hermitage Museum, Leningrad. (George Roos/Art Resource,
New York)

## PASTORAL

1906, by Henri Matisse (French, 1869–1954). Oil on canvas.
Museum of Modern Art of the City of Paris. (Art Resource,
New York)

MATISSE  A Postcard Book™
© *1989 by Running Press Book Publishers*

Henri-Matisse

*STILL LIFE WITH RED CARPET*
1906, by Henri Matisse (French, 1869–1954). Oil on canvas.
Museum of Painting and Sculpture, Grenoble. (Scala/Art
Resource, New York)

*LUXURY I*
1907, by Henri Matisse (French, 1869–1954). Oil on canvas.
National Museum of Modern Art, Paris. (Giraudon/Art
Resource, New York)

*HARMONY IN RED*
1908, by Henri Matisse (French, 1869–1954). Oil on canvas.
Hermitage Museum, Leningrad. (George Roos/Art Resource,
New York)

*THE DIVAN*
by Henri Matisse (French, 1869–1954). Musée de l'Orangérie,
Paris. (Art Resource, New York)

## PORTRAIT OF MADAME MATISSE

1913, by Henri Matisse (French, 1869–1954). Oil on canvas.
Hermitage Museum, Leningrad. (George Roos/Art Resource,
New York)

MATISSE  A Postcard Book™
© 1989 by Running Press Book Publishers

*INTERIOR WITH GOLDFISH*
1914, by Henri Matisse (French, 1869–1954). Oil on canvas.
National Museum of Modern Art, Paris. (Giraudon/Art
Resource, New York)

MATISSE  A Postcard Book™
© *1989 by Running Press Book Publishers*

## APPLES

1916, by Henri Matisse (French, 1869–1954). Oil on canvas, 116.9 × 88.9 cm, Gift of Mrs. Wolfgang Schoenborn and Samuel A. Marx. © 1989 The Art Institute of Chicago. All Rights Reserved.

*TREE NEAR TRIVAUX POND*
1916–1917, by Henri Matisse (French, 1869–1954). Oil on canvas. Tate Gallery, London. (Art Resource, New York)

## BATHERS BY A RIVER

1916–1917, by Henri Matisse (French, 1869–1954). Oil on canvas, 259.7 × 389.9 cm, Charles H. and Mary F. Worcester Collection. © 1989 The Art Institute of Chicago. All Rights Reserved.

## THE PLASTER TORSO

1919, by Henri Matisse (French, 1869–1954). Oil on canvas.
Museum of Art, São Paulo. (Giraudon/Art Resource,
New York)

MATISSE  A Postcard Book™
© 1989 by Running Press Book Publishers

## MISS MATISSE AND MISS DERICARER / INTERIOR AT NICE

1920, by Henri Matisse (French, 1869–1954). Oil on canvas. Musée de l'Annonciade, Saint Tropez. (Giraudon/Art Resource, New York)

MATISSE  A Postcard Book™
© 1989 by Running Press Book Publishers

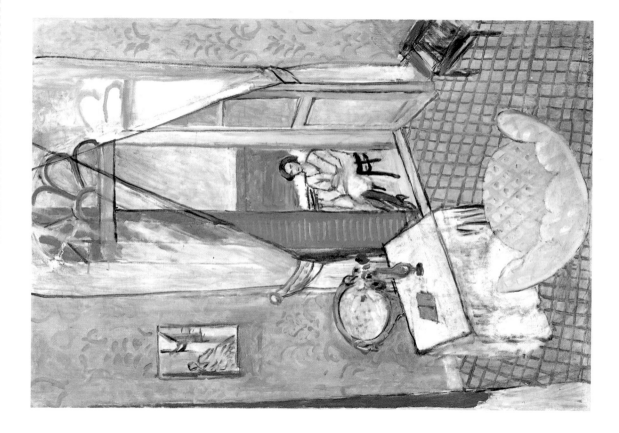

## INTERIOR AT NICE

1921, by Henri Matisse (French, 1869–1954). Oil on canvas, 132.2 × 88.1 cm, Gift of Mrs. Gilbert W. Chapman. © 1989 The Art Institute of Chicago. All Rights Reserved.

## WOMAN BEFORE AN AQUARIUM

1921–1923, by Henri Matisse (French, 1869–1954). Oil on canvas, 80.7 × 100 cm, Helen Birch Bartlett Memorial Collection. © 1989 The Art Institute of Chicago. All Rights Reserved.

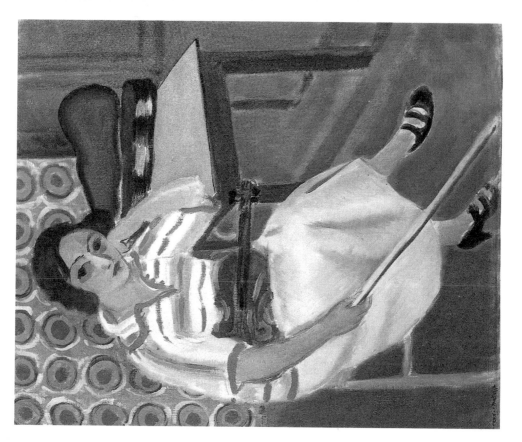

*WOMAN WITH VIOLIN*

1921–1923, by Henri Matisse (French, 1869–1954). Oil on canvas. Musée de l'Orangérie, Paris. (Scala/Art Resource, New York)

MATISSE  A Postcard Book™
© *1989 by Running Press Book Publishers*

## ODALISQUE IN RED TROUSERS

1922, by Henri Matisse (French, 1869–1954). Oil on canvas. National Museum of Modern Art, Paris. (Giraudon/Art Resource, New York)

MATISSE  A Postcard Book™
© 1989 by Running Press Book Publishers

*DECORATIVE FIGURE AGAINST*
*AN ORNAMENTAL BACKGROUND*
c. 1927, by Henri Matisse (French, 1869–1954). Oil on canvas.
National Museum of Modern Art, Paris. (Giraudon/Art
Resource, New York)

MATISSE A Postcard Book™
© *1989 by Running Press Book Publishers*

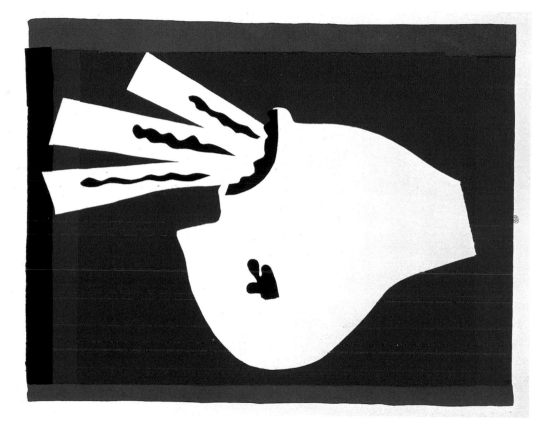

## *THE CLOWN,* FROM *JAZZ*

1938, by Henri Matisse (French, 1869–1954). Stencil print
after a paper-cut maquette. School of Fine Arts, Paris.
(Giraudon/Art Resource, New York)

## READER AGAINST A
## BLACK BACKGROUND

1939, by Henri Matisse (French, 1869–1954). Oil on canvas.
National Museum of Modern Art, Paris. (Giraudon/Art
Resource, New York)

## STILL LIFE WITH MAGNOLIA
1941, by Henri Matisse (French, 1869–1954). Oil on canvas.
National Museum of Modern Art, Paris. (Giraudon/Art
Resource, New York)

## SEATED DANCER

1942, by Henri Matisse (French, 1869–1954). Museum of Modern Art of the City of Paris. (Giraudon/Art Resource, New York)

MATISSE  A Postcard Book™
© 1989 by Running Press Book Publishers

*STILL LIFE WITH LARGE COPPER VASE*
by Henri Matisse (French, 1869–1954). Private collection.
(Art Resource, New York)

un moment
di libres.
Ne devrait-on
pas faire ac-
complir un
grand voyage
en avion aux
jeunes gens
ayant terminé
leurs études.

## *ICARUS,* FROM *JAZZ*

1943, by Henri Matisse (French, 1869–1954). Stencil print after a paper-cut maquette. The Estate of Matisse. (Art Resource, New York)

*STILL LIFE WITH POMEGRANATES*
1947, by Henri Matisse (French, 1869–1954). Oil on canvas.
Matisse Museum, Nice. (Giraudon/Art Resource, New York)

MATISSE  A Postcard Book™
© *1989 by Running Press Book Publishers*

## BLUE NUDE III

1952, by Henri Matisse (French, 1869–1954). Cut and pasted
paper. Private collection. (Giraudon/Art Resource, New York)

MATISSE  A Postcard Book™
© 1989 by Running Press Book Publishers

## THE SNAIL

1953, by Henri Matisse (French, 1869–1954). Gouache on cut and pasted paper. Tate Gallery, London. (Art Resource, New York)